Mining the Mind of

KING SOLOMON

Godly wisdom for all occasions.

DR. STEVEN A. JIRGAL

CORE™

The Core Media Group, Inc.
www.thecoremediagroup.com

Published by The Core Media Group, Inc., P.O. Box 2037, Indian Trail, NC 28079.

Printed in the United States of America.

Note: This is a categorized collection of King Solomon's and his contemporary's proverbs. Many of these proverbs can fall into more than one category. The attempt is made to place each proverb in the category that seems best suited for it. The following verses are taken from The New American Standard version of the Bible.

TABLE OF CONTENTS

Introduction

INTRODUCTION

King Solomon is noted as the greatest man who ever lived in terms of material wealth and wisdom. He ruled in Jerusalem for forty years. Even today, when a person possesses superior intellect he is referred to as having Solomonic wisdom. The Bible records that Solomon possessed a multitude of horses, 1,400 chariots, 12,000 horsemen, land, houses, and slaves in abundance. He made silver, and gold as common as stones. (I Chronicles 1:14-15). It's easy to see why men lead expeditions to locate his hidden treasures. A find like that would ensure financial security for generations to come. Solomon not only surpassed his peers in material wealth, but in wisdom as well. II Chronicles 9:22 states, "So King Solomon became greater than all the kings of the earth in riches and wisdom.

This is all in fulfillment of a promise God made to him. One night while Solomon lay on his bed the Lord appeared to him and said, "ask what I shall give you." (II Chron. 1:7). He could have asked for any number of things. He could have requested long life, wealth, popularity, great exploits, victory over his enemies, or expansion of his territories. But he asked for wisdom to rule over the people of God. God not only granted Solomon's request, but also blessed him with riches and honor. He was to be the wealthiest and wisest of all men. (II Chronicles 1:10-12). And as Solomon measured his life, he stated that wisdom is a commodity worth chasing. He likened wisdom to silver and gold. He said,

"How blessed is the man who finds wisdom
And the man who gains understanding.
For her profit is better than the profit of silver
And her gain better than fine gold.
She is more precious than jewels;

And nothing you desire compares with her.
Long life is in her right hand;
In her left hand are riches and honor.
Her ways are pleasant ways
And all her paths are peace.
She is a tree of life to those who take hold of her,
And happy are all who hold her fast.
Take my instruction and not silver,
And knowledge rather than choicest gold.
For wisdom is better than jewels;
And all desirable things cannot compare with her.
My fruit is better than gold, even pure gold,
And my yield *better* than choicest silver."(Prov. 3:13-18,
8:10-11,19)

King Solomon felt that the gaining of wisdom was far greater
than the gaining of wealth. In fact, he ascribed no less than
185 verses to the gaining of wisdom as compared to 29
verses to the gaining and handling of wealth.

The manuscript you hold is a treasure map of sorts. It
carries the wisdom of Solomon which he gained from the
experiences his wealth afforded him. Solomon's purpose in
compiling these proverbs is clearly found in the opening six
verses of his book,

"The proverbs of Solomon the son of David, king of Israel:
To know wisdom and instruction,
To discern the sayings of understanding,
To receive instruction in wise behavior,
Righteousness, justice and equity;
To give prudence to the naive,
To the youth knowledge and discretion,
A wise man will hear and increase in learning,
And a man of understanding will acquire wise counsel,
To understand a proverb and a figure,
The words of the wise and their riddles."

These sayings are certain to give you the wisdom needed to succeed in various aspects of life. And while the list is far from exhaustive, it is quite full. The topics addressed range from integrity to marriage to interpersonal relations and beyond. Because of his position and wealth King Solomon was able to experience a plethora of activities the world of his time had to offer.

In Eccl. 2:1-10 Solomon notes that he explored and experimented in various areas of life to increase his knowledge and understanding. These areas include but are not limited to: pleasure, building, horticulture, irrigation systems, animal husbandry, financial investments, and sexual exploits. He engaged in every, and any activity his hand and mind could bring him to. He was "all in" and held nothing back. As a result of all his activities, you and I are the beneficiaries of the totality of his life.

A fool is easy to spot. He seems to be perpetually broke, bruised, battling, and blaming. He never seems to learn from his mistakes, he just repeats them over and over again. A smart person is one who makes mistakes and learns from them. But the truly wise is one who observes the mistakes of others and learns from them. Thus he avoids much of the pain life delivers from poor decisions.

Be wise! Learn from King Solomon! He made mistakes and ventured time and again into the world of experience. He observed others and added to his wisdom. It must be noted that not all the proverbs recorded can be attributed to King Solomon. He had peers who carried such wisdom so as to compel Solomon to include their bits of wisdom with him.

A word of caution:

What you are about to read are proverbs not promises. These are tendencies not guarantees. If you try to formulate your life by simply implementing these proverbs, you may very well find yourself disappointed and discouraged. Just as a train rides on parallel rails, these proverbs can provide support and stability to your life. They are meant to be "guard rails" keeping your life balanced and on track. Read on and grow in wisdom and understanding!

MINING THE MIND OF KING SOLOMON

GODLY WISDOM FOR ALL OCCASIONS

BALANCE

30:7
Two things I asked of You, do not refuse me before I die:

30:8
Keep deception and lies far from me, give me neither poverty nor riches; Feed me with the food that is my portion,

30:9
That I not be full and deny *You* and say, "Who is the Lord?" or that I not be in want and steal, and profane the name of my God.

COMMUNICATION

4:24
Put away from you a deceitful mouth and put devious speech far from you.

10:11
The mouth of the righteous is a fountain of life, but the mouth of the wicked conceals violence.

10:14
Wise men store up knowledge, but with the mouth of the foolish, ruin is at hand.

10:18
He who conceals hatred *has* lying lips, and he who spreads slander is a fool.

10:19
When there are many words, transgression is unavoidable, but he who restrains his lips is wise.

10:20
The tongue of the righteous is *as* choice silver, the heart of the wicked is *worth* little.

10:21
The lips of the righteous feed many, but fools die for lack of understanding.

11:13
He who goes about as a talebearer reveals secrets, but he who is trustworthy conceals a matter.

12:14
A man will be satisfied with good by the fruit of his words, and the deeds of a man's hands will return to him.

12:17
He who speaks truth tells what is right, but a false witness, deceit.

12:18
There is one who speaks rashly like the thrusts of a sword, but the tongue of the wise brings healing.

12:19
Truthful lips will be established forever, but a lying tongue is only for a moment.

13:2
From the fruit of a man's mouth he enjoys good, but the desire of the treacherous is violence.

13:3
The one who guards his mouth preserves his life; The one who opens wide his lips comes to ruin.

14:3
In the mouth of the foolish is a rod for *his* back, but the lips

of the wise will protect them.

15:1
A gentle answer turns away wrath, but a harsh word stirs up anger.

15:2
The tongue of the wise makes knowledge acceptable, but the mouth of fools spouts folly.

15:4
A soothing tongue is a tree of life, but perversion in it crushes the spirit.

15:23
A man has joy in an apt answer, and how delightful is a timely word!

15:26
Evil plans are an abomination to the Lord, but pleasant words are pure.

16:21
The wise in heart will be called understanding, and sweetness of speech increases persuasiveness.

16:24
Pleasant words are a honeycomb, sweet to the soul and healing to the bones.

16:27
A worthless man digs up evil, while his words are like scorching fire.

16:28
A perverse man spreads strife, and a slanderer separates intimate friends.

17:20
He who has a crooked mind finds no good, and he who is perverted in his language falls into evil.

18:6
A fool's lips bring strife, and his mouth calls for blows.

18:7
A fool's mouth is his ruin, and his lips are the snare of his soul.

18:8
The words of a whisperer are like dainty morsels, and they go down into the innermost parts of the body.

18:20
With the fruit of a man's mouth his stomach will be satisfied; he will be satisfied *with* the product of his lips.

18:21
Death and life are in the power of the tongue, and those who love it will eat its fruit.

20:19
He who goes about as a slanderer reveals secrets, therefore do not associate with a gossip.

21:23
He who guards his mouth and his tongue, guards his soul from troubles.

25:11
Like apples of gold in settings of silver is a word spoken in right circumstances.

25:15
By forbearance a ruler may be persuaded, and a soft tongue breaks the bone.

25:23
The north wind brings forth rain, and a backbiting tongue, an angry countenance.

26:28
A lying tongue hates those it crushes, and a flattering mouth works ruin.

29:20
Do you see a man who is hasty in his words? there is more hope for a fool than for him.

30:14
There is a kind of *man* whose teeth are *like* swords and his jaw teeth *like* knives, to devour the afflicted from the earth and the needy from among men.

DILIGENCE/DISCIPLINE

6:6
Go to the ant, O sluggard, observe her ways and be wise,

6:7
Which, having no chief, officer or ruler,

6:8
Prepares her food in the summer *and* gathers her provision in the harvest.

10:4
Poor is he who works with a negligent hand, but the hand of the diligent makes rich.

10:5
He who gathers in summer is a son who acts wisely, *but* he who sleeps in harvest is a son who acts shamefully.

10:26
Like vinegar to the teeth and smoke to the eyes, so is the lazy one to those who send him.

12:1
Whoever loves discipline loves knowledge, but he who hates reproof is stupid.

12:11
He who tills his land will have plenty of bread, but he who pursues worthless *things* lacks sense.

12:24
The hand of the diligent will rule, but the slack *hand* will be put to forced labor.

12:27
A lazy man does not roast his prey, but the precious possession of a man *is* diligence.

13:4
The soul of the sluggard craves and *gets* nothing, but the soul of the diligent is made fat.

13:17
A wicked messenger falls into adversity, but a faithful envoy *brings* healing.

13:18
Poverty and shame *will come* to him who neglects discipline, but he who regards reproof will be honored.

14:4
Where no oxen are, the manger is clean, but much revenue *comes* by the strength of the ox.

14:23
In all labor there is profit, but mere talk *leads* only to poverty.

15:19
The way of the lazy is as a hedge of thorns, but the path of the upright is a highway.

15:32
He who neglects discipline despises himself, But he who listens to reproof acquires understanding.

16:26
A worker's appetite works for him, for his hunger urges him *on*.

18:9
He also who is slack in his work is brother to him who destroys.

19:15
Laziness casts into a deep sleep, and an idle man will suffer hunger.

19:24
The sluggard buries his hand in the dish *but* will not even bring it back to his mouth.

19:27
Cease listening, my son, to discipline and *you will* stray from the words of knowledge.

20:4
The sluggard does not plow after the autumn, so he begs during the harvest and has nothing.

20:13
Do not love sleep, or you will become poor; open your eyes, *and* you will be satisfied with food.

21:5
The plans of the diligent *lead* surely to advantage, but every-

one who is hasty *comes* surely to poverty.

21:17
He who loves pleasure *will become* a poor man; he who loves wine and oil will not become rich.

21:25
The desire of the sluggard puts him to death, for his hands refuse to work;

21:26
All day long he is craving, while the righteous gives and does not hold back.

22:13
The sluggard says, "There is a lion outside; I will be killed in the streets!"

22:29
Do you see a man skilled in his work? he will stand before kings; he will not stand before obscure men.

24:10
If you are slack in the day of distress, your strength is limited.

24:27
Prepare your work outside and make it ready for yourself in the field; Afterwards, then, build your house.

24:30
I passed by the field of the sluggard And by the vineyard of the man lacking sense,

24:31
And behold, it was completely overgrown with thistles; its surface was covered with nettles, and its stone wall was broken down.

24:32
When I saw, I reflected upon it; I looked, *and* received instruction.

24:33
"A little sleep, a little slumber, a little folding of the hands to rest,"

24:34
Then your poverty will come *as* a robber and your want like an armed man.

25:16
Have you found honey? Eat *only* what you need, that you not have it in excess and vomit it.

25:28
Like a city that is broken into *and* without walls is a man who has no control over his spirit.

26:13
The sluggard says, "There is a lion in the road! a lion is in the open square!"

26:14
As the door turns on its hinges, so *does* the sluggard on his bed.

26:15
The sluggard buries his hand in the dish; he is weary of bringing it to his mouth again.

26:16
The sluggard is wiser in his own eyes than seven men who can give a discreet answer.

27:7
A sated man loathes honey, but to a famished man any bit-

ter thing is sweet.

27:18
He who tends the fig tree will eat its fruit, and he who cares for his master will be honored.

27:23
Know well the condition of your flocks, *and* pay attention to your herds;

27:24
For riches are not forever, nor does a crown *endure* to all generations.

27:25
When the grass disappears, the new growth is seen, and the herbs of the mountains are gathered in,

27:26
The lambs *will be* for your clothing, and the goats *will bring* the price of a field,

27:27
And *there will be* goats' milk enough for your food, for the food of your household, And sustenance for your maidens.

28:19
He who tills his land will have plenty of food, But he who follows empty *pursuits* will have poverty in plenty.

31:13
She looks for wool and flax and works with her hands in delight.

31:14
She is like merchant ships; she brings her food from afar.

31:16
She considers a field and buys it; from her earnings she plants a vineyard.

31:17
She girds herself with strength and makes her arms strong.

31:18
She senses that her gain is good; her lamp does not go out at night.

31:19
She stretches out her hands to the distaff, and her hands grasp the spindle.

31:21
She is not afraid of the snow for her household, for all her household are clothed with scarlet.

31:22
She makes coverings for herself; her clothing is fine linen and purple.

31:24
She makes linen garments and sells *them*, and supplies belts to the tradesmen.

31:25
Strength and dignity are her clothing, and she smiles at the future.

31:27
She looks well to the ways of her household, and does not eat the bread of idleness.

31:31
Give her the product of her hands, and let her works praise her in the gates.

DISCERNMENT/DISCRETION

2:11
Discretion will guard you, understanding will watch over you,

2:12
To deliver you from the way of evil, from the man who speaks perverse things;

2:13
From those who leave the paths of uprightness to walk in the ways of darkness;

2:14
Who delight in doing evil and rejoice in the perversity of evil;

2:15
Whose paths are crooked, and who are devious in their ways;

2:16
To deliver you from the strange woman, from the adulteress who flatters with her words;

2:17
That leaves the companion of her youth and forgets the covenant of her God;

2:18
For her house sinks down to death and her tracks *lead* to the dead;

2:19
None who go to her return again, nor do they reach the paths of life.

5:1
My son, give attention to my wisdom, incline your ear to my understanding;

5:2
That you may observe discretion and your lips may reserve knowledge.

6:30
Men do not despise a thief if he steals to satisfy himself when he is hungry;

6:31
But when he is found, he must repay sevenfold; he must give all the substance of his house.

10:13
On the lips of the discerning, wisdom is found, but a rod is for the back of him who lacks understanding.

11:22
As a ring of gold in a swine's snout so is a beautiful woman who lacks discretion.

12:23
A prudent man conceals knowledge, but the heart of fools proclaims folly.

13:7
There is one who pretends to be rich, but has nothing; another pretends to be poor, but has great wealth.

16:14
The fury of a king is *like* messengers of death, but a wise man will appease it.

16:17
The highway of the upright is to depart from evil; he who

watches his way preserves his life.

17:4
An evildoer listens to wicked lips; a liar pays attention to a destructive tongue.

17:28
Even a fool, when he keeps silent, is considered wise; when he closes his lips, he is *considered* prudent.

18:13
He who gives an answer before he hears, it is folly and shame to him.

19:11
A man's discretion makes him slow to anger, and it is his glory to overlook a transgression.

23:1
When you sit down to dine with a ruler, consider carefully what is before you,

23:2
and put a knife to your throat if you are a man of *great* appetite.

23:3
Do not desire his delicacies, for it is deceptive food.

23:6
Do not eat the bread of a selfish man, or desire his delicacies;

23:7
For as he thinks within himself, so he is. He says to you, "Eat and drink!" But his heart is not with you.

23:8
You will vomit up the morsel you have eaten, and waste your compliments.

23:26
Give me your heart, my son, and let your eyes delight in my ways.

23:27
For a harlot is a deep pit and an adulterous woman is a narrow well.

23:28
Surely she lurks as a robber, and increases the faithless among men.

23:29
Who has woe? Who has sorrow? Who has contentions? Who has complaining? Who has wounds without cause? Who has redness of eyes?

23:30
Those who linger long over wine, those who go to taste mixed wine.

23:31
Do not look on the wine when it is red, when it sparkles in the cup, when it goes down smoothly;

23:32
At the last it bites like a serpent and stings like a viper.

23:33
Your eyes will see strange things and your mind will utter perverse things.

23:34
And you will be like one who lies down in the middle of the

sea, or like one who lies down on the top of a mast.

23:35
"They struck me, *but* I did not become ill; they beat me, *but* I did not know *it*. When shall I awake? I will seek another drink."

30:32
If you have been foolish in exalting yourself or if you have plotted *evil*, *put your* hand on your mouth.

EMOTIONS

4:23
Watch over your heart with all diligence, for from it *flow* the springs of life.

10:12
Hatred stirs up strife, but love covers all transgressions.

12:16
A fool's anger is known at once, but a prudent man conceals dishonor.

12:25
Anxiety in a man's heart weighs it down, but a good word makes it glad.

13:12
Hope deferred makes the heart sick, but desire fulfilled is a tree of life.

14:10
The heart knows its own bitterness, and a stranger does not share its joy.

14:13
Even in laughter the heart may be in pain, and the end of joy may be grief.

14:17
A quick-tempered man acts foolishly, and a man of evil devices is hated.

14:29
He who is slow to anger has great understanding, but he who is quick-tempered exalts folly.

14:30
A tranquil heart is life to the body, but passion is rottenness to the bones.

15:13
A joyful heart makes a cheerful face, but when the heart is sad, the spirit is broken.

15:15
All the days of the afflicted are bad, but a cheerful heart *has* a continual feast.

15:17
Better is a dish of vegetables where love is than a fattened ox *served* with hatred.

15:18
A hot-tempered man stirs up strife, but the slow to anger calms a dispute.

15:30
Bright eyes gladden the heart; good news puts fat on the bones.

16:15
In the light of a king's face is life, and his favor is like a cloud

with the spring rain.

16:32
He who is slow to anger is better than the mighty, and he who rules his spirit, than he who captures a city.

17:14
The beginning of strife is *like* letting out water, so abandon the quarrel before it breaks out.

17:22
A joyful heart is good medicine, but a broken spirit dries up the bones.

17:27
He who restrains his words has knowledge, and he who has a cool spirit is a man of understanding.

18:14
The spirit of a man can endure his sickness, but as *for* a broken spirit who can bear it?

19:12
The king's wrath is like the roaring of a lion, but his favor is like dew on the grass.

19:19
A man of great anger will bear the penalty, for if you rescue *him*, you will only have to do it again.

20:2
The terror of a king is like the growling of a lion; he who provokes him to anger forfeits his own life.

22:24
Do not associate with a man *given* to anger; or go with a hot-tempered man,

22:25
Or you will learn his ways and find a snare for yourself.

25:25
Like cold water to a weary soul, so is good news from a distant land.

27:20
Sheol and Abaddon are never satisfied, nor are the eyes of man ever satisfied.

29:11
A fool always loses his temper, but a wise man holds it back.

29:22
An angry man stirs up strife, and a hot-tempered man abounds in transgression.

30:33
For the churning of milk produces butter, and pressing the nose brings forth blood; so the churning of anger produces strife.

FAMILY

1:8
Hear, my son, your father's instruction and do not forsake your mother's teaching;

1:9
Indeed, they are a graceful wreath to your head and ornaments about your neck.

6:20
My son, observe the commandment of your father and do not forsake the teaching of your mother;

6:21
Bind them continually on your heart; tie them around your neck.

6:22
When you walk about, they will guide you; when you sleep, they will watch over you; and when you awake, they will talk to you.

10:1
A wise son makes a father glad, but a foolish son is a grief to his mother.

11:29
He who troubles his own house will inherit wind, and the foolish will be servant to the wise hearted.

13:24
He who withholds his rod hates his son, but he who loves him disciplines him diligently.

14:1
The wise woman builds her house, but the foolish tears it down with her own hands.

15:5
A fool rejects his father's discipline, but he who regards reproof is sensible.

15:20
A wise son makes a father glad, but a foolish man despises his mother.

17:1
Better is a dry morsel and quietness with it than a house full of feasting with strife.

17:6
Grandchildren are the crown of old men, and the glory of sons is their fathers.

17:25
A foolish son is a grief to his father and bitterness to her who bore him.

19:13
A foolish son is destruction to his father, and the contentions of a wife are a constant dripping.

19:14
House and wealth are an inheritance from fathers, but a prudent wife is from the Lord.

19:18
Discipline your son while there is hope, and do not desire his death.

19:26
He who assaults *his* father *and* drives *his* mother away is a shameful and disgraceful son.

20:20
He who curses his father or his mother, his lamp will go out in time of darkness.

20:30
Stripes that wound scour away evil, and strokes *reach* the innermost parts.

21:9
It is better to live in a corner of a roof than in a house shared with a contentious woman.

21:19
It is better to live in a desert land than with a contentious

and vexing woman.

22:6
Train up a child in the way he should go, even when he is old he will not depart from it.

22:15
Foolishness is bound up in the heart of a child; the rod of discipline will remove it far from him.

23:22
Listen to your father who begot you, and do not despise your mother when she is old.

25:24
It is better to live in a corner of the roof than in a house shared with a contentious woman.

27:8
Like a bird that wanders from her nest, so is a man who wanders from his home.

28:24
He who robs his father or his mother and says, "It is not a transgression," is the companion of a man who destroys.

29:15
The rod and reproof give wisdom, but a child who gets his own way brings shame to his mother.

29:17
Correct your son, and he will give you comfort; he will also delight your soul.

30:11
There is a kind of *man* who curses his father and does not bless his mother.

30:17
The eye that mocks a father and scorns a mother, the ravens of the valley will pick it out, and the young eagles will eat it.

31:28
Her children rise up and bless her; her husband *also*, and he praises her, *saying*:

31:29
"Many daughters have done nobly, but you excel them all."

FATHERLY ADVICE

2:1
My son, if you will receive my word and treasure my commandments within you,

2:2
Make your ear attentive to wisdom, incline your heart to understanding;

2:3
For if you cry for discernment, lift your voice for understanding;

2:4
If you seek her as silver and search for her as for hidden treasures;

2:5
Then you will discern the fear of the Lord and discover the knowledge of God.

2:6
For the Lord gives wisdom; from His mouth *come* knowledge and understanding.

2:7
He stores up sound wisdom for the upright; *He is* a shield to those who walk in integrity,

2:8
Guarding the paths of justice, and He preserves the way of His godly ones.

2:9
Then you will discern righteousness and justice and equity *and* every good course.

2:10
For wisdom will enter your heart and knowledge will be pleasant to your soul;

3:1
My son, do not forget my teaching, but let your heart keep my commandments;

3:2
For length of days and years of life and peace they will add to you.

4:1
Hear, O sons, the instruction of a father, and give attention that you may gain understanding,

4:2
for I give you sound teaching; do not abandon my instruction.

4:3
When I was a son to my father, tender and the only son in the sight of my mother,

4:4
then he taught me and said to me, "Let your heart hold fast

GODLY WISDOM FOR ALL OCCASIONS

my words; keep my commandments and live;

4:10
Hear, my son, and accept my sayings and the years of your life will be many.

4:11
I have directed you in the way of wisdom; I have led you in upright paths.

4:12
When you walk, your steps will not be impeded; and if you run, you will not stumble.

4:13
Take hold of instruction; do not let go. Guard her, for she is your life.

4:20
My son, give attention to my words; incline your ear to my sayings.

4:21
Do not let them depart from your sight; keep them in the midst of your heart.

4:22
For they are life to those who find them and health to all their body.

13:1
A wise son *accepts his* father's discipline, but a scoffer does not listen to rebuke.

23:13
Do not hold back discipline from the child, although you strike him with the rod, he will not die.

23:14
You shall strike him with the rod and rescue his soul from Sheol.

23:15
My son, if your heart is wise, my own heart also will be glad;

23:16
And my inmost being will rejoice when your lips speak what is right.

23:19
Listen, my son, and be wise, and direct your heart in the way.

23:24
The father of the righteous will greatly rejoice, and he who sires a wise son will be glad in him.

23:25
Let your father and your mother be glad, and let her rejoice who gave birth to you.

24:13
My son, eat honey, for it is good, yes, the honey from the comb is sweet to your taste;

27:19
As in water face *reflects* face, so the heart of man *reflects* man.

FINANCES

6:1
My son, if you have become surety for your neighbor, have given a pledge for a stranger,

6:2
If you have been snared with the words of your mouth, have been caught with the words of your mouth,

6:3
Do this then, my son, and deliver yourself; since you have come into the hand of your neighbor, go, humble yourself, and importune your neighbor.

6:4
Give no sleep to your eyes, nor slumber to your eyelids;

6:5
Deliver yourself like a gazelle from *the hunter's* hand and like a bird from the hand of the fowler.

10:2
Ill-gotten gains do not profit, but righteousness delivers from death.

10:15
The rich man's wealth is his fortress, the ruin of the poor is their poverty.

10:22
It is the blessing of the Lord that makes rich, and He adds no sorrow to it.

11:15
He who is guarantor for a stranger will surely suffer for it, but he who hates being a guarantor is secure.

13:8
The ransom of a man's life is his wealth, but the poor hears no rebuke.

13:11
Wealth *obtained* by fraud dwindles, but the one who gathers

by labor increases *it*.

13:22
A good man leaves an inheritance to his children's children, and the wealth of the sinner is stored up for the righteous.

14:20
The poor is hated even by his neighbor, but those who love the rich are many.

17:18
A man lacking in sense pledges and becomes guarantor in the presence of his neighbor.

18:11
A rich man's wealth is his strong city, and like a high wall in his own imagination.

18:23
The poor man utters supplications, but the rich man answers roughly.

19:4
Wealth adds many friends, but a poor man is separated from his friend.

19:7
All the brothers of a poor man hate him; how much more do his friends abandon him! He pursues *them with* words, *but* they are gone.

20:16
Take his garment when he becomes surety for a stranger; and for foreigners, hold him in pledge.

20:21
An inheritance gained hurriedly at the beginning will not be blessed in the end.

22:7
The rich rules over the poor, and the borrower *becomes* the lender's slave.

22:16
He who oppresses the poor to make more for himself or who gives to the rich, *will* only *come to* poverty.

22:26
Do not be among those who give pledges, among those who become guarantors for debts.

22:27
If you have nothing with which to pay, why should he take your bed from under you?

23:4
Do not weary yourself to gain wealth, cease from your consideration *of it.*

23:5
When you set your eyes on it, it is gone. For *wealth* certainly makes itself wings like an eagle that flies *toward* the heavens.

28:8
He who increases his wealth by interest and usury gathers it for him who is gracious to the poor.

28:20
A faithful man will abound with blessings, but he who makes haste to be rich will not go unpunished.

28:22
A man with an evil eye hastens after wealth and does not know that want will come upon him.

FOCUS

4:25
Let your eyes look directly ahead and let your gaze be fixed straight in front of you.

4:26
Watch the path of your feet and all your ways will be established.

4:27
Do not turn to the right nor to the left; turn your foot from evil.

13:19
Desire realized is sweet to the soul, but it is an abomination to fools to turn away from evil.

GENEROSITY

3:27
Do not withhold good from those to whom it is due, when it is in your power to do *it*.

3:28
Do not say to your neighbor, "Go, and come back, and tomorrow I will give *it*," when you have it with you.

11:24
There is one who scatters, and yet increases all the more, and there is one who withholds what is justly due, *and yet it results* only in want.

11:25
The generous man will be prosperous, and he who waters

will himself be watered.

11:26
He who withholds grain, the people will curse him, but blessing will be on the head of him who sells *it*.

14:21
He who despises his neighbor sins, but happy is he who is gracious to the poor.

14:31
He who oppresses the poor taunts his Maker, but he who is gracious to the needy honors Him.

19:6
Many will seek the favor of a generous man, and every man is a friend to him who gives gifts.

19:17
One who is gracious to a poor man lends to the Lord, and He will repay him for his good deed.

21:13
He who shuts his ear to the cry of the poor will also cry himself and not be answered.

22:9
He who is generous will be blessed, for he gives some of his food to the poor.

24:11
Deliver those who are being taken away to death, and those who are staggering to slaughter, oh hold *them* back.

28:27
He who gives to the poor will never want, but he who shuts his eyes will have many curses.

30:15
The leech has two daughters, "Give," "Give." There are three things that will not be satisfied, four that will not say, "Enough":

30:16
Sheol, and the barren womb, earth that is never satisfied with water, and fire that never says, "Enough."

31:15
She rises also while it is still night and gives food to her household and portions to her maidens.

31:20
She extends her hand to the poor, and she stretches out her hands to the needy.

GODLINESS

1:7
The fear of the Lord is the beginning of knowledge; fools despise wisdom and instruction.

2:20
So you will walk in the way of good men and keep to the paths of the righteous.

2:21
For the upright will live in the land and the blameless will remain in it;

2:22
But the wicked will be cut off from the land and the treacherous will be uprooted from it.

3:32
For the devious are an abomination to the Lord; but He is intimate with the upright.

3:33
The curse of the Lord is on the house of the wicked, but He blesses the dwelling of the righteous.

10:6
Blessings are on the head of the righteous, but the mouth of the wicked conceals violence.

10:7
The memory of the righteous is blessed, but the name of the wicked will rot.

10:16
The wages of the righteous is life, the income of the wicked, punishment.

10:23
Doing wickedness is like sport to a fool, and so is wisdom to a man of understanding.

10:24
What the wicked fears will come upon him, but the desire of the righteous will be granted.

10:25
When the whirlwind passes, the wicked is no more, but the righteous has an everlasting foundation.

10:28
The hope of the righteous is gladness, but the expectation of the wicked perishes.

10:29
The way of the Lord is a stronghold to the upright, but ruin

to the workers of iniquity.

10:30
The righteous will never be shaken, but the wicked will not dwell in the land.

10:31
The mouth of the righteous flows with wisdom, but the perverted tongue will be cut out.

10:32
The lips of the righteous bring forth what is acceptable, but the mouth of the wicked what is perverted.

11:4
Riches do not profit in the day of wrath, but righteousness delivers from death.

11:5
The righteousness of the blameless will smooth his way, but the wicked will fall by his own wickedness.

11:6
The righteousness of the upright will deliver them, but the treacherous will be caught by *their own* greed.

11:7
When a wicked man dies, *his* expectation will perish, and the hope of strong men perishes.

11:8
The righteous is delivered from trouble, but the wicked takes his place.

11:9
With *his* mouth the godless man destroys his neighbor, but through knowledge the righteous will be delivered.

11:11
By the blessing of the upright a city is exalted, but by the mouth of the wicked it is torn down.

11:18
The wicked earns deceptive wages, but he who sows righteousness *gets* a true reward.

11:19
He who is steadfast in righteousness *will attain* to life, and he who pursues evil *will bring about* his own death.

11:20
The perverse in heart are an abomination to the Lord, but the blameless in *their* walk are His delight.

11:21
Assuredly, the evil man will not go unpunished, but the descendants of the righteous will be delivered.

11:23
The desire of the righteous is only good *but* the expectation of the wicked is wrath.

11:27
He who diligently seeks good seeks favor, but he who seeks evil, evil will come to him.

11:28
He who trusts in his riches will fall, but the righteous will flourish like the *green* leaf.

11:30
The fruit of the righteous is a tree of life, and he who is wise wins souls.

11:31
If the righteous will be rewarded in the earth, how much

more the wicked and the sinner!

12:2
A good man will obtain favor from the Lord, but He will condemn a man who devises evil.

12:3
A man will not be established by wickedness, but the root of the righteous will not be moved.

12:5
The thoughts of the righteous are just *but* the counsels of the wicked are deceitful.

12:6
The words of the wicked lie in wait for blood, but the mouth of the upright will deliver them.

12:7
The wicked are overthrown and are no more, but the house of the righteous will stand.

12:10
A righteous man has regard for the life of his animal, but *even* the compassion of the wicked is cruel.

12:12
The wicked man desires the booty of evil men, but the root of the righteous yields *fruit*.

12:13
An evil man is ensnared by the transgression of his lips, but the righteous will escape from trouble.

12:21
No harm befalls the righteous, but the wicked are filled with trouble.

12:26
The righteous is a guide to his neighbor, but the way of the wicked leads them astray.

12:28
In the way of righteousness is life, and in *its* pathway there is no death.

13:5
A righteous man hates falsehood, but a wicked man acts disgustingly and shamefully.

13:6
Righteousness guards the one whose way is blameless, but wickedness subverts the sinner.

13:21
Adversity pursues sinners, but the righteous will be rewarded with prosperity.

13:25
The righteous has enough to satisfy his appetite, but the stomach of the wicked is in need.

14:2
He who walks in his uprightness fears the Lord, but he who is devious in his ways despises Him.

14:11
The house of the wicked will be destroyed, but the tent of the upright will flourish.

14:14
The backslider in heart will have his fill of his own ways, but a good man will *be satisfied* with his.

14:19
The evil will bow down before the good, and the wicked at

the gates of the righteous.

14:32
The wicked is thrust down by his wrongdoing, but the righteous has a refuge when he dies.

14:34
Righteousness exalts a nation, but sin is a disgrace to *any* people.

15:6
Great wealth is *in* the house of the righteous, but trouble is in the income of the wicked.

15:8
The sacrifice of the wicked is an abomination to the Lord, but the prayer of the upright is His delight.

15:9
The way of the wicked is an abomination to the Lord, but He loves one who pursues righteousness.

15:28
The heart of the righteous ponders how to answer, but the mouth of the wicked pours out evil things.

15:29
The Lord is far from the wicked, but He hears the prayer of the righteous.

16:7
When a man's ways are pleasing to the Lord, He makes even his enemies to be at peace with him.

16:8
Better is a little with righteousness than great income with injustice.

16:31
A gray head is a crown of glory; it is found in the way of righteousness.

19:16
He who keeps the commandment keeps his soul *but* he who is careless of conduct will die.

20:9
Who can say, "I have cleansed my heart, I am pure from my sin"?

21:3
To do righteousness and justice is desired by the Lord more than sacrifice.

21:7
The violence of the wicked will drag them away, because they refuse to act with justice.

21:12
The righteous one considers the house of the wicked, turning the wicked to ruin.

21:18
The wicked is a ransom for the righteous, and the treacherous is in the place of the upright.

21:21
He who pursues righteousness and loyalty finds life, righteousness and honor.

21:27
The sacrifice of the wicked is an abomination, how much more when he brings it with evil intent!

21:29
A wicked man displays a bold face, but as for the upright, he

makes his way sure.

22:5
Thorns *and* snares are in the way of the perverse; he who guards himself will be far from them.

22:8
He who sows iniquity will reap vanity, and the rod of his fury will perish.

23:17
Do not let your heart envy sinners, but *live* in the fear of the Lord always.

23:18
Surely there is a future, and your hope will not be cut off.

24:8
One who plans to do evil, men will call a schemer.

24:9
The devising of folly is sin, and the scoffer is an abomination to men.

24:15
Do not lie in wait, O wicked man, against the dwelling of the righteous; do not destroy his resting place;

24:16
For a righteous man falls seven times, and rises again, but the wicked stumble in *time of* calamity.

24:24
He who says to the wicked, "You are righteous," peoples will curse him, nations will abhor him;

24:25
But to those who rebuke the *wicked* will be delight, and a

good blessing will come upon them.

24:26
He kisses the lips who gives a right answer.

24:29
Do not say, "Thus I shall do to him as he has done to me; I will render to the man according to his work."

25:26
Like a trampled spring and a polluted well is a righteous man who gives way before the wicked.

28:1
The wicked flee when no one is pursuing, but the righteous are bold as a lion.

28:4
Those who forsake the law praise the wicked, but those who keep the law strive with them.

28:5
Evil men do not understand justice, but those who seek the Lord understand all things.

28:9
He who turns away his ear from listening to the law, even his prayer is an abomination.

28:10
He who leads the upright astray in an evil way will himself fall into his own pit, but the blameless will inherit good.

28:12
When the righteous triumph, there is great glory, but when the wicked rise, men hide themselves.

28:13
He who conceals his transgressions will not prosper, but he who confesses and forsakes *them* will find compassion.

28:18
He who walks blamelessly will be delivered, but he who is crooked will fall all at once.

28:28
When the wicked rise, men hide themselves; but when they perish, the righteous increase.

29:6
By transgression an evil man is ensnared, but the righteous sings and rejoices.

29:7
The righteous is concerned for the rights of the poor, the wicked does not understand *such* concern.

29:10
Men of bloodshed hate the blameless, but the upright are concerned for his life.

29:16
When the wicked increase, transgression increases; but the righteous will see their fall.

29:18
Where there is no vision, the people are unrestrained, but happy is he who keeps the law.

29:27
An unjust man is abominable to the righteous, and he who is upright in the way is abominable to the wicked.

31:30
Charm is deceitful and beauty is vain, *but* a woman who

fears the Lord, she shall be praised.

HUMILITY

11:2
When pride comes, then comes dishonor, but with the humble is wisdom.

14:16
A wise man is cautious and turns away from evil, but a fool is arrogant and careless.

15:10
Grievous punishment is for him who forsakes the way; he who hates reproof will die.

15:25
The Lord will tear down the house of the proud, but He will establish the boundary of the widow.

15:31
He whose ear listens to the life-giving reproof will dwell among the wise.

15:33
The fear of the Lord is the instruction for wisdom, and before honor *comes* humility.

16:5
Everyone who is proud in heart is an abomination to the Lord; assuredly, he will not be unpunished.

16:18
Pride *goes* before destruction, and a haughty spirit before stumbling.

16:19
It is better to be humble in spirit with the lowly than to divide the spoil with the proud.

18:12
Before destruction the heart of man is haughty, but humility *goes* before honor.

21:4
Haughty eyes and a proud heart, the lamp of the wicked, is sin.

21:24
"Proud," "Haughty," "Scoffer," are his names, who acts with insolent pride.

22:4
The reward of humility *and* the fear of the Lord are riches, honor and life.

22:27
It is not good to eat much honey, nor is it glory to search out one's own glory.

25:6
Do not claim honor in the presence of the king, and do not stand in the place of great men;

25:7
For it is better that it be said to you, "Come up here," than for you to be placed lower in the presence of the prince, whom your eyes have seen.

26:12
Do you see a man wise in his own eyes? there is more hope for a fool than for him.

27:1
Do not boast about tomorrow, for you do not know what a day may bring forth.

27:2
Let another praise you, and not your own mouth; a stranger, and not your own lips.

27:21
The crucible is for silver and the furnace for gold, and each *is tested* by the praise accorded him.

28:14
How blessed is the man who fears always, but he who hardens his heart will fall into calamity.

28:25
An arrogant man stirs up strife, but he who trusts in the Lord will prosper.

29:23
A man's pride will bring him low, but a humble spirit will obtain honor.

30:1
The words of Agur the son of Jakeh, the oracle.
The man declares to Ithiel, to Ithiel and Ucal:

30:2
Surely I am more stupid than any man, and I do not have the understanding of a man.

30:3
Neither have I learned wisdom, nor do I have the knowledge of the Holy One.

30:12
There is a kind who is pure in his own eyes, yet is not

washed from his filthiness.

30:13
There is a kind—oh how lofty are his eyes! And his eyelids are raised *in arrogance.*

30:18
There are three things which are too wonderful for me, four which I do not understand:

30:19
The way of an eagle in the sky, the way of a serpent on a rock, the way of a ship in the middle of the sea, and the way of a man with a maid.

30:20
This is the way of an adulterous woman: she eats and wipes her mouth, and says, "I have done no wrong."

INTEGRITY

10:9
He who walks in integrity walks securely, but he who perverts his ways will be found out.

10:10
He who winks the eye causes trouble, and a babbling fool will be ruined.

11:3
The integrity of the upright will guide them, but the crookedness of the treacherous will destroy them.

15:11
A just balance and scales belong to the Lord; all the weights of the bag are His concern.

15:27
He who profits illicitly troubles his own house, but he who hates bribes will live.

17:8
A bribe is a charm in the sight of its owner; wherever he turns, he prospers.

17:23
A wicked man receives a bribe from the bosom to pervert the ways of justice.

19:1
Better is a poor man who walks in his integrity than he who is perverse in speech and is a fool.

19:28
A rascally witness makes a mockery of justice, and the mouth of the wicked spreads iniquity.

20:6
Many a man proclaims his own loyalty, but who can find a trustworthy man?

20:7
A righteous man who walks in his integrity—How blessed are his sons after him.

20:10
Differing weights and differing measures, both of them are abominable to the Lord.

20:11
It is by his deeds that a lad distinguishes himself if his conduct is pure and right.

20:14
"Bad, bad," says the buyer, but when he goes his way, then

he boasts.

20:17
Bread obtained by falsehood is sweet to a man, but afterward his mouth will be filled with gravel.

20:25
It is a trap for a man to say rashly, "It is holy!" and after the vows to make inquiry.

21:8
The way of a guilty man is crooked, but as for the pure, his conduct is upright.

22:28
Do not move the ancient boundary which your fathers have set.

23:10
Do not move the ancient boundary or go into the fields of the fatherless,

23:11
For their Redeemer is strong; He will plead their case against you.

25:13
Like the cold of snow in the time of harvest is a faithful messenger to those who send him, for he refreshes the soul of his masters.

25:19
Like a bad tooth and an unsteady foot is confidence in a faithless man in time of trouble.

26:2
Like a sparrow in *its* flitting, like a swallow in *its* flying, so a curse without cause does not alight.

28:6
Better is the poor who walks in his integrity than he who is crooked though he be rich.

29:4
The king gives stability to the land by justice, but a man who takes bribes overthrows it.

29:24
He who is a partner with a thief hates his own life; he hears the oath but tells nothing.

30:10
Do not slander a slave to his master, or he will curse you and you will be found guilty.

INTERPERSONAL RELATIONSHIPS

3:3
Do not let kindness and truth leave you; bind them around your neck, write them on the tablet of your heart.

3:4
So you will find favor and good repute in the sight of God and man.

3:29
Do not devise harm against your neighbor, while he lives securely beside you.

3:30
Do not contend with a man without cause, if he has done you no harm.

3:31
Do not envy a man of violence and do not choose any of his

ways.

4:14
Do not enter the path of the wicked and do not proceed in the way of evil men.

4:15
Avoid it, do not pass by it; turn away from it and pass on.

4:16
For they cannot sleep unless they do evil; and they are robbed of sleep unless they make *someone* stumble.

4:17
For they eat the bread of wickedness and drink the wine of violence.

4:18
But the path of the righteous is like the light of dawn, that shines brighter and brighter until the full day.

4:19
The way of the wicked is like darkness; they do not know over what they stumble.

6:12
A worthless person, a wicked man, is the one who walks with a perverse mouth,

6:13
Who winks with his eyes, who signals with his feet, who points with his fingers;

6:14
Who *with* perversity in his heart continually devises evil, who spreads strife.

6:15
Therefore his calamity will come suddenly; instantly he will be broken and there will be no healing.

9:7
He who corrects a scoffer gets dishonor for himself, and he who reproves a wicked man *gets* insults for himself.

9:8
Do not reprove a scoffer, or he will hate you, reprove a wise man and he will love you.

9:9
Give *instruction* to a wise man and he will be still wiser, teach a righteous man and he will increase *his* learning.

11:10
When it goes well with the righteous, the city rejoices, and when the wicked perish, there is joyful shouting.

11:12
He who despises his neighbor lacks sense, but a man of understanding keeps silent.

11:16
A gracious woman attains honor, and ruthless men attain riches.

11:17
The merciful man does himself good, but the cruel man does himself harm.

16:29
A man of violence entices his neighbor and leads him in a way that is not good.

17:9
He who conceals a transgression seeks love, but he who

repeats a matter separates intimate friends.

17:17
A friend loves at all times, and a brother is born for adversity.

17:19
He who loves transgression loves strife; he who raises his door seeks destruction.

18:1
He who separates himself seeks *his own* desire, he quarrels against all sound wisdom.

18:3
When a wicked man comes, contempt also comes, and with dishonor *comes* scorn.

18:16
A man's gift makes room for him and brings him before great men.

18:19
A brother offended *is harder to be won* than a strong city, and contentions are like the bars of a citadel.

18:24
A man of *too many* friends *comes* to ruin, but there is a friend who sticks closer than a brother.

20:3
Keeping away from strife is an honor for a man, but any fool will quarrel.

20:29
The glory of young men is their strength, and the honor of old men is their gray hair.

21:10
The soul of the wicked desires evil; his neighbor finds no favor in his eyes.

21:14
A gift in secret subdues anger, and a bribe in the bosom, strong wrath.

22:10
Drive out the scoffer, and contention will go out, even strife and dishonor will cease.

23:20
Do not be with heavy drinkers of wine, *or* with gluttonous eaters of meat;

23:21
For the heavy drinker and the glutton will come to poverty, and drowsiness will clothe *one* with rags.

24:1
Do not be envious of evil men, nor desire to be with them;

24:2
For their minds devise violence, and their lips talk of trouble.

24:17
Do not rejoice when your enemy falls, and do not let your heart be glad when he stumbles;

24:18
Or the Lord will see *it* and be displeased, and turn His anger away from him.

25:8
Do not go out hastily to argue *your case*; otherwise, what will you do in the end, when your neighbor humiliates you?

25:9
Argue your case with your neighbor, and do not reveal the secret of another,

25:10
Or he who hears *it* will reproach you, and the evil report about you will not pass away.

25:17
Let your foot rarely be in your neighbor's house, or he will become weary of you and hate you.

25:20
Like one who takes off a garment on a cold day, *or like* vinegar on soda, is he who sings songs to a troubled heart.

25:21
If your enemy is hungry, give him food to eat; and if he is thirsty, give him water to drink;

25:22
For you will heap burning coals on his head, and the Lord will reward you.

26:17
Like one who takes a dog by the ears is he who passes by *and* meddles with strife not belonging to him.

26:18
Like a madman who throws firebrands, arrows and death,

26:19
So is the man who deceives his neighbor, and says, "Was I not joking?"

26:20
For lack of wood the fire goes out, and where there is no whisperer, contention quiets down.

26:21
Like charcoal to hot embers and wood to fire, so is a contentious man to kindle strife.

26:22
The words of a whisperer are like dainty morsels, and they go down into the innermost parts of the body.

26:23
Like an earthen vessel overlaid with silver dross are burning lips and a wicked heart.

26:24
He who hates disguises *it* with his lips, but he lays up deceit in his heart.

26:25
When he speaks graciously, do not believe him, for there are seven abominations in his heart.

26:26
Though his hatred covers itself with guile, his wickedness will be revealed before the assembly.

26:27
He who digs a pit will fall into it, and he who rolls a stone, it will come back on him.

27:3
A stone is heavy and the sand weighty, but the provocation of a fool is heavier than both of them.

27:4
Wrath is fierce and anger is a flood, but who can stand before jealousy?

27:5
Better is open rebuke than love that is concealed.

27:6
Faithful are the wounds of a friend, but deceitful are the kisses of an enemy.

27:9
Oil and perfume make the heart glad, so a man's counsel is sweet to his friend.

27:10
Do not forsake your own friend or your father's friend, and do not go to your brother's house in the day of your calamity; better is a neighbor who is near than a brother far away.

27:13
Take his garment when he becomes surety for a stranger; and for an adulterous woman hold him in pledge.

27:14
He who blesses his friend with a loud voice early in the morning, it will be reckoned a curse to him.

27:15
A constant dripping on a day of steady rain and a contentious woman are alike;

27:16
He who would restrain her restrains the wind, and grasps oil with his right hand.

27:17
Iron sharpens iron, so one man sharpens another.

28:3
A poor man who oppresses the lowly is *like* a driving rain which leaves no food.

28:7
He who keeps the law is a discerning son, but he who is a

companion of gluttons humiliates his father.

28:11
The rich man is wise in his own eyes, but the poor who has understanding sees through him.

28:17
A man who is laden with the guilt of human blood will be a fugitive until death; let no one support him.

28:21
To show partiality is not good, because for a piece of bread a man will transgress.

28:23
He who rebukes a man will afterward find *more* favor than he who flatters with the tongue.

29:5
A man who flatters his neighbor is spreading a net for his steps.

29:21
He who pampers his slave from childhood will in the end find him to be a son.

31:1
The words of King Lemuel, the oracle which his mother taught him:

31:2
What, O my son? and what, O son of my womb? and what, O son of my vows?

31:3
Do not give your strength to women, or your ways to that which destroys kings.

31:6
Give strong drink to him who is perishing, and wine to him whose life is bitter.

31:7
Let him drink and forget his poverty and remember his trouble no more.

LEADERSHIP

11:14
Where there is no guidance the people fall, but in abundance of counselors there is victory.

14:28
In a multitude of people is a king's glory, but in the dearth of people is a prince's ruin.

15:22
Without consultation, plans are frustrated, but with many counselors they succeed.

16:12
It is an abomination for kings to commit wicked acts, for a throne is established on righteousness.

16:10
A divine decision is in the lips of the king; his mouth should not err in judgment.

16:13
Righteous lips are the delight of kings, and he who speaks right is loved.

17:7
Excellent speech is not fitting for a fool, much less are lying

lips to a prince.

17:15
He who justifies the wicked and he who condemns the righteous, both of them alike are an abomination to the Lord.

17:26
It is also not good to fine the righteous, *nor* to strike the noble for *their* uprightness.

18:5
To show partiality to the wicked is not good, *nor* to thrust aside the righteous in judgment.

18:17
The first to plead his case *seems* right, *until* another comes and examines him.

20:8
A king who sits on the throne of justice disperses all evil with his eyes.

20:18
Prepare plans by consultation, and make war by wise guidance.

20:26
A wise king winnows the wicked, and drives the *threshing* wheel over them.

21:15
The exercise of justice is joy for the righteous, but is terror to the workers of iniquity.

24:6
For by wise guidance you will wage war, and in abundance of counselors there is victory.

24:23
These also are sayings of the wise. To show partiality in judgment is not good.

25:1
These also are proverbs of Solomon which the men of Hezekiah, king of Judah, transcribed.

25:2
It is the glory of God to conceal a matter, but the glory of kings is to search out a matter.

25:3
As the heavens for height and the earth for depth, so the heart of kings is unsearchable.

25:4
Take away the dross from the silver, and there comes out a vessel for the smith;

25:5
Take away the wicked before the king, and his throne will be established in righteousness.

28:15
Like a roaring lion and a rushing bear is a wicked ruler over a poor people.

28:16
A leader who is a great oppressor lacks understanding, *but* he who hates unjust gain will prolong *his* days.

29:2
When the righteous increase, the people rejoice, but when a wicked man rules, people groan.

29:12
If a ruler pays attention to falsehood, all his ministers *be-*

come wicked.

29:14

If a king judges the poor with truth, his throne will be established forever.

30:29

There are three things which are stately in *their* march, even four which are stately when they walk:

30:30

The lion *which* is mighty among beasts and does not retreat before any,

30:31

The strutting rooster, the male goat also, and a king *when his* army is with him.

31:4

It is not for kings, O Lemuel, it is not for kings to drink wine, or for rulers to desire strong drink,

31:5

For they will drink and forget what is decreed, and pervert the rights of all the afflicted.

31:8

Open your mouth for the mute, for the rights of all the unfortunate.

31:9

Open your mouth, judge righteously, and defend the rights of the afflicted and needy.

MARRIAGE

5:15
Drink water from your own cistern and fresh water from your own well.

12:4
An excellent wife is the crown of her husband, but she who shames *him* is like rottenness in his bones.

15:16
Should your springs be dispersed abroad, streams of water in the streets?

15:17
Let them be yours alone and not for strangers with you.

15:18
Let your fountain be blessed, and rejoice in the wife of your youth.

15:19
As a loving hind and a graceful doe, let her breasts satisfy you at all times; be exhilarated always with her love.

15:20
For why should you, my son, be exhilarated with an adulteress and embrace the bosom of a foreigner?

18:22
He who finds a wife finds a good thing and obtains favor from the Lord.

31:10
An excellent wife, who can find? for her worth is far above jewels.

31:11
The heart of her husband trusts in her, and he will have no lack of gain.

31:12
She does him good and not evil all the days of her life.

PEER PRESSURE

1:10
My son, if sinners entice you, do not consent.

1:11
If they say, "Come with us, let us lie in wait for blood, let us ambush the innocent without cause;

1:12
Let us swallow them alive like Sheol, even whole, as those who go down to the pit;

1:13
We will find all *kinds* of precious wealth, we will fill our houses with spoil;

1:14
Throw in your lot with us, we shall all have one purse,"

1:15
My son, do not walk in the way with them. Keep your feet from their path,

1:16
For their feet run to evil and they hasten to shed blood.

1:17
Indeed, it is useless to spread the *baited* net in the sight of

any bird;

1:18
But they lie in wait for their own blood; they ambush their own lives.

1:19
So are the ways of everyone who gains by violence; it takes away the life of its possessors.

13:20
He who walks with wise men will be wise, but the companion of fools will suffer harm.

PURITY

5:3
For the lips of an adulteress drip honey and smoother than oil is her speech;

5:4
But in the end she is bitter as wormwood, sharp as a two-edged sword.

5:5
Her feet go down to death, her steps take hold of Sheol.

5:6
She does not ponder the path of life; her ways are unstable, she does not know *it*.

5:7
Now then, *my* sons, listen to me and do not depart from the words of my mouth.

5:8
Keep your way far from her and do not go near the door of her house,

5:9
Or you will give your vigor to others and your years to the cruel one;

5:10
And strangers will be filled with your strength and your hard-earned goods *will go* to the house of an alien;

5:11
And you groan at your final end, when your flesh and your body are consumed;

5:12
And you say, "How I have hated instruction! and my heart spurned reproof!

5:13
"I have not listened to the voice of my teachers, nor inclined my ear to my instructors!

5:14
"I was almost in utter ruin in the midst of the assembly and congregation."

6:23
For the commandment is a lamp and the teaching is light; and reproofs for discipline are the way of life.

6:24
To keep you from the evil woman, from the smooth tongue of the adulteress.

6:25
Do not desire her beauty in your heart, nor let her capture

you with her eyelids.

6:26
For on account of a harlot *one is reduced* to a loaf of bread, and an adulteress hunts for the precious life.

6:27
Can a man take fire in his bosom and his clothes not be burned?

6:28
Or can a man walk on hot coals and his feet not be scorched?

6:29
So is the one who goes in to his neighbor's wife; whoever touches her will not go unpunished.

6:32
The one who commits adultery with a woman is lacking sense; he who would destroy himself does it.

6:33
Wounds and disgrace he will find, and his reproach will not be blotted out.

6:34
For jealousy enrages a man, and he will not spare in the day of vengeance.

6:35
He will not accept any ransom, nor will he be satisfied though you give many gifts.

7:5
That they may keep you from an adulteress, from the foreigner who flatters with her words.

7:6
For at the window of my house I looked out through my lattice,

7:7
And I saw among the naive, *and* discerned among the youth A young man lacking sense,

7:8
passing through the street near her corner; and he takes the way to her house,

7:9
in the twilight, in the evening, in the middle of the night and *in* the darkness.

7:10
And behold, a woman *comes* to meet him, dressed as a harlot and cunning of heart.

7:11
She is boisterous and rebellious, her feet do not remain at home;

7:12
She is now in the streets, now in the squares, and lurks by every corner.

7:13
So she seizes him and kisses him and with a brazen face she says to him:

7:14
"I was due to offer peace offerings; today I have paid my vows.

7:15
"Therefore I have come out to meet you, to seek your pres-

ence earnestly, and I have found you.

7:16
"I have spread my couch with coverings, with colored linens of Egypt.

7:17
"I have sprinkled my bed with myrrh, aloes and cinnamon.

7:18
"Come, let us drink our fill of love until morning; let us delight ourselves with caresses.

7:19
"For my husband is not at home, he has gone on a long journey;

7:20
He has taken a bag of money with him, at the full moon he will come home."

7:21
With her many persuasions she entices him; with her flattering lips she seduces him.

7:22
Suddenly he follows her as an ox goes to the slaughter, or as *one in* fetters to the discipline of a fool.

7:23
Until an arrow pierces through his liver; as a bird hastens to the snare, so he does not know that it *will cost him* his life.

7:24
Now therefore, *my* sons, listen to me, and pay attention to the words of my mouth.

7:25
Do not let your heart turn aside to her ways, do not stray into her paths.

7:26
For many are the victims she has cast down, and numerous are all her slain.

7:27
Her house is the way to Sheol, descending to the chambers of death.

22:11
He who loves purity of heart *and* whose speech is gracious, the king is his friend.

22:14
The mouth of an adulteress is a deep pit; he who is cursed of the Lord will fall into it.

REPUTATION

12:8
A man will be praised according to his insight, but one of perverse mind will be despised.

12:9
Better is he who is lightly esteemed and has a servant than he who honors himself and lacks bread

13:7
There is one who pretends to be rich, but has nothing; *another* pretends to be poor, but has great wealth.

13:9
The light of the righteous rejoices, but the lamp of the

wicked goes out.

22:1
A *good* name is to be more desired than great wealth, favor is better than silver and gold.

25:14
Like clouds and wind without rain is a man who boasts of his gifts falsely.

31:23
Her husband is known in the gates, when he sits among the elders of the land.

REVERANCE

3:7
Do not be wise in your own eyes; fear the Lord and turn away from evil.

3:8
It will be healing to your body and refreshment to your bones.

3:9
Honor the Lord from your wealth and from the first of all your produce;

3:10
So your barns will be filled with plenty and your vats will overflow with new wine.

3:11
My son, do not reject the discipline of the Lord or loathe His reproof,

3:12
For whom the Lord loves He reproves, even as a father *corrects* the son in whom he delights.

8:13
"The fear of the Lord is to hate evil; pride and arrogance and the evil way and the perverted mouth, I hate.

9:10
The fear of the Lord is the beginning of wisdom, and the knowledge of the Holy One is understanding.

9:11
For by me your days will be multiplied, and years of life will be added to you.

10:27
The fear of the Lord prolongs life, and the years of the wicked will be shortened.

13:13
The one who despises the word will be in debt to it, but the one who fears the commandment will be rewarded.

14:26
In the fear of the Lord there is strong confidence, and his children will have refuge.

14:27
The fear of the Lord is a fountain of life, that one may avoid the snares of death.

15:16
Better is a little with the fear of the Lord than great treasure and turmoil with it.

16:6
By lovingkindness and truth iniquity is atoned for, and by the

fear of the Lord one keeps away from evil.

19:23
The fear of the Lord *leads* to life, so that one may sleep satisfied, untouched by evil.

SIN

5:21
For the ways of a man are before the eyes of the Lord, and He watches all his paths.

5:22
His own iniquities will capture the wicked, and he will be held with the cords of his sin.

5:23
He will die for lack of instruction, and in the greatness of his folly he will go astray.

11:1
A false balance is an abomination to the Lord, but a just weight is His delight.

13:23
Abundant food *is in* the fallow ground of the poor, but it is swept away by injustice.

14:9
Fools mock at sin, but among the upright there is good will.

SOVEREIGNTY OF GOD

3:5
Trust in the Lord with all your heart and do not lean on your own understanding.

3:6
In all your ways acknowledge Him, and He will make your paths straight.

3:19
The Lord by wisdom founded the earth, by understanding He established the heavens.

3:20
By His knowledge the deeps were broken up and the skies drip with dew.

3:25
Do not be afraid of sudden fear nor of the onslaught of the wicked when it comes;

3:26
For the Lord will be your confidence and will keep your foot from being caught.

6:16
There are six things which the Lord hates, yes, seven which are an abomination to Him:

6:17
Haughty eyes, a lying tongue, and hands that shed innocent blood.

6:18
a heart that devises wicked plans, feet that run rapidly toe evil,

6:19
a false witness who utter lies, and one who spreads strife among brothers.

10:3
The Lord will not allow the righteous to hunger, but He will reject the craving of the wicked.

15:3
The eyes of the Lord are in every place, watching the evil and the good.

15:11
Sheol and Abaddon *lie open* before the Lord, how much more the hearts of men!

16:1
The plans of the heart belong to man, but the answer of the tongue is from the Lord.

16:2
All the ways of a man are clean in his own sight, but the Lord weighs the motives.

16:4
The Lord has made everything for its own purpose, even the wicked for the day of evil.

16:9
The mind of man plans his way, but the Lord directs his steps.

16:3
Commit your works to the Lord and your plans will be established.

16:20
He who gives attention to the word will find good, and

blessed is he who trusts in the Lord.

16:33
The lot is cast into the lap, but its every decision is from the Lord.

17:3
The refining pot is for silver and the furnace for gold, but the Lord tests hearts.

17:5
He who mocks the poor taunts his Maker; he who rejoices at calamity will not go unpunished.

17:11
A rebellious man seeks only evil, so a cruel messenger will be sent against him.

17:13
He who returns evil for good, evil will not depart from his house.

18:10
The name of the Lord is a strong tower; the righteous runs into it and is safe.

18:18
The *cast* lot puts an end to strife and decides between the mighty ones.

19:21
Many plans are in a man's heart, but the counsel of the Lord will stand.

20:12
The hearing ear and the seeing eye, the Lord has made both of them.

20:22
Do not say, "I will repay evil"; wait for the Lord, and He will save you.

20:24
Man's steps are *ordained* by the Lord, how then can man understand his way?

20:27
The spirit of man is the lamp of the Lord, searching all the innermost parts of his being.

21:1
The king's heart is *like* channels of water in the hand of the Lord; He turns it wherever He wishes.

21:2
Every man's way is right in his own eyes, but the Lord weighs the hearts.

21:30
There is no wisdom and no understanding and no counsel against the Lord.

21:31
The horse is prepared for the day of battle, but victory belongs to the Lord.

22:2
The rich and the poor have a common bond, the Lord is the maker of them all.

22:12
The eyes of the Lord preserve knowledge, but He overthrows the words of the treacherous man.

22:22
Do not rob the poor because he is poor, or crush the af-

flicted at the gate;

22:23
For the Lord will plead their case and take the life of those who rob them.

24:12
If you say, "See, we did not know this," does He not consider *it* who weighs the hearts? And does He not know *it* who keeps your soul? And will He not render to man according to his work?

24:19
Do not fret because of evildoers or be envious of the wicked;

24:20
For there will be no future for the evil man; the lamp of the wicked will be put out.

24:21
My son, fear the Lord and the king; do not associate with those who are given to change,

24:22
For their calamity will rise suddenly, and who knows the ruin *that comes* from both of them?

29:13
The poor man and the oppressor have this in common: the Lord gives light to the eyes of both.

29:26
Many seek the ruler's favor, but justice for man *comes* from the Lord.

29:25
The fear of man brings a snare, but he who trusts in the Lord

will be exalted.

30:4
Who has ascended into heaven and descended? Who has gathered the wind in His fists? Who has wrapped the waters in His garment? Who has established all the ends of the earth? What is His name or His son's name? Surely you know!

30:5
Every word of God is tested; He is a shield to those who take refuge in Him.

30:6
Do not add to His words or He will reprove you, and you will be proved a liar.

30:21
Under three things the earth quakes, and under four, it cannot bear up:

30:22
Under a slave when he becomes king, and a fool when he is satisfied with food,

30:23
Under an unloved woman when she gets a husband, and a maidservant when she supplants her mistress.

3:34
Though He scoffs at the scoffers, yet He gives grace to the afflicted.

TRUTH

12:20
Deceit is in the heart of those who devise evil, but counselors of peace have joy.

12:22
Lying lips are an abomination to the Lord, but those who deal faithfully are His delight.

14:5
A trustworthy witness will not lie, but a false witness utters lies.

14:22
Will they not go astray who devise evil? But kindness and truth *will be to* those who devise good.

14:25
A truthful witness saves lives, but he who utters lies is treacherous.

16:30
He who winks his eyes *does so* to devise perverse things; he who compresses his lips brings evil to pass.

19: 22
What is desirable in a man is his kindness, and *it is* better to be a poor man than a liar.

19:5
A false witness will not go unpunished, and he who tells lies will not escape.

19:9
A false witness will not go unpunished, and he who tells lies will perish.

20:23
Differing weights are an abomination to the Lord, and a false scale is not good.

20:28
Loyalty and truth preserve the king, and he upholds his throne by righteousness.

21:6
The acquisition of treasures by a lying tongue is a fleeting vapor, the pursuit of death.

21:28
A false witness will perish, but the man who listens *to the truth* will speak forever.

24:28
Do not be a witness against your neighbor without cause, and do not deceive with your lips.

25:18
Like a club and a sword and a sharp arrow is a man who bears false witness against his neighbor.

WISDOM

1:1
The proverbs of Solomon the son of David, king of Israel:

1:2 To know wisdom and instruction, to discern the sayings of understanding,

1:3
To receive instruction in wise behavior, righteousness, justice and equity;

1:4
To give prudence to the naive, to the youth knowledge and discretion,

1:5
a wise man will hear and increase in learning, and a man of understanding will acquire wise counsel,

1:6
to understand a proverb and a figure, the words of the wise and their riddles.

1:20
Wisdom shouts in the street, she lifts her voice in the square;

1:21
At the head of the noisy *streets* she cries out; at the entrance of the gates in the city she utters her sayings:

1:22
"How long, O naive ones, will you love being simple-minded? and scoffers delight themselves in scoffing and fools hate knowledge?

1:23
"Turn to my reproof, behold, I will pour out my spirit on you; I will make my words known to you.

1:24
"Because I called and you refused, I stretched out my hand and no one paid attention;

1:25
And you neglected all my counsel and did not want my reproof;

1:26
I will also laugh at your calamity; I will mock when your dread comes,

1:27
when your dread comes like a storm and your calamity comes a whirlwind, when distress and anguish come upon you.

1:28
"Then they will call on me, but I will not answer they will seek me diligently but they will not find me,

1:29
because they hated knowledge and did not choose the fear of the Lord.

1:30
They would not accept my counsel, they spurned all my reproof.

1:31
So they shall eat of the fruit of their own way and be satiated with their own devices.

1:32
For the waywardness of the naive will kill them, and the complacency of fools will destroy them.

1:33
But he who listens to me shall live securely and will be at ease from the dread of evil.

3:13
How blessed is the man who finds wisdom and the man who gains understanding.

3:14
For her profit is better than the profit of silver and her gain better than fine gold.

3:15
She is more precious than jewels; and nothing you desire compares with her.

3:16
Long life is in her right hand; in her left hand are riches and honor.

3:17
Her ways are pleasant ways and all her paths are peace.

3:18
She is a tree of life to those who take hold of her, and happy are all who hold her fast.

3:21
My son, let them not vanish from your sight; keep sound wisdom and discretion,

3:22
so they will be life to your soul and adornment to your neck.

3:23
8:1Then you will walk in your way securely and your foot will not stumble.

3:24
When you lie down, you will not be afraid; when you lie down, your sleep will be sweet.

3:35
The wise will inherit honor, but fools display dishonor.

4:5
Acquire wisdom! Acquire understanding! do not forget nor turn away from the words of my mouth.

4:6
"Do not forsake her, and she will guard you; love her, and she will watch over you.

4:7
The beginning of wisdom *is*: Acquire wisdom; and with all your acquiring, get understanding.

4:8
Prize her, and she will exalt you; she will honor you if you embrace her.

4:9
She will place on your head a garland of grace; she will present you with a crown of beauty.

7:1
My son, keep my words and treasure my commandments within you.

7:2
Keep my commandments and live, and my teaching as the apple of your eye.

7:3
Bind them on your fingers; write them on the tablet of your heart.

7:4
Say to wisdom, "You are my sister," and call understanding *your* intimate friend;

8:1
Does not wisdom call, and understanding lift up her voice?

8:2
On top of the heights beside the way, where the paths meet, she takes her stand;

8:3
Beside the gates, at the opening to the city, at the entrance of the doors, she cries out:

8:4
"To you, O men, I call, and my voice is to the sons of men.

8:5
"O naive ones, understand prudence; and, O fools, understand wisdom.

8:6
"Listen, for I will speak noble things; and the opening of my lips *will reveal* right things.

8:7
"For my mouth will utter truth; and wickedness is an abomination to my lips.

8:8
"All the utterances of my mouth are in righteousness; there is nothing crooked or perverted in them.

8:9
"They are all straightforward to him who understands, and right to those who find knowledge.

8:10
"Take my instruction and not silver, and knowledge rather than choicest gold.

8:11
"For wisdom is better than jewels; and all desirable things cannot compare with her.

8:12
"I, wisdom, dwell with prudence, and I find knowledge *and* discretion.

8:14
"Counsel is mine and sound wisdom; I am understanding, power is mine.

8:15
"By me kings reign, and rulers decree justice.

8:16
"By me princes rule, and nobles, all who judge rightly.

8:17
"I love those who love me; and those who diligently seek me will find me.

8:18
"Riches and honor are with me, enduring wealth and righteousness.

8:19
"My fruit is better than gold, even pure gold, and my yield *better* than choicest silver.

8:20
"I walk in the way of righteousness, in the midst of the paths of justice,

8:21
To endow those who love me with wealth, that I may fill their treasuries.

8:22
"The Lord possessed me at the beginning of His way, before His works of old.

8:23
"From everlasting I was established, from the beginning, from the earliest times of the earth.

8:24
"When there were no depths I was brought forth, when there were no springs abounding with water.

8:25
"Before the mountains were settled, before the hills I was brought forth;

8:26
While He had not yet made the earth and the fields, nor the first dust of the world.

8:27
"When He established the heavens, I was there, when He inscribed a circle on the face of the deep,

8:28
when He made firm the skies above, when the springs of the deep became fixed,

8:29
when He set for the sea its boundary so that the water would not transgress His command, when He marked out the foundations of the earth;

8:30
Then I was beside Him, *as* a master workman; and I was daily *His* delight, rejoicing always before Him,

8:31
rejoicing in the world, His earth, and *having* my delight in the sons of men.

8:32

"Now therefore, O sons, listen to me, for blessed are they who keep my ways.

8:33

"Heed instruction and be wise, and do not neglect it.

8:34

"Blessed is the man who listens to me, watching daily at my gates, waiting at my doorposts.

8:35

"For he who finds me finds life and obtains favor from the Lord.

8:36

"But he who sins against me injures himself; all those who hate me love death."

9:1

Wisdom has built her house, she has hewn out her seven pillars;

9:2

She has prepared her food, she has mixed her wine; she has also set her table;

9:3

She has sent out her maidens, she calls from the tops of the heights of the city:

9:4

"Whoever is naive, let him turn in here!" To him who lacks understanding she says,

9:5

"Come, eat of my food and drink of the wine I have mixed.

9:6
"Forsake *your* folly and live, and proceed in the way of understanding."

9:12
If you are wise, you are wise for yourself, and if you scoff, you alone will bear it.

9:13
The woman of folly is boisterous, *she is* naive and knows nothing.

9:14
She sits at the doorway of her house, on a seat by the high places of the city,

9:15
Calling to those who pass by, who are making their paths straight:

9:16
"Whoever is naive, let him turn in here," and to him who lacks understanding she says,

9:17
"Stolen water is sweet; and bread *eaten* in secret is pleasant."

9:18
But he does not know that the dead are there, *that* her guests are in the depths of Sheol.

10:1
A wise son makes a father glad, but a foolish son is a grief to his mother.

10:8
The wise of heart will receive commands, but a babbling fool

will be ruined.

10:17
He is *on* the path of life who heeds instruction, but he who ignores reproof goes astray.

12:15
The way of a fool is right in his own eyes, but a wise man is he who listens to counsel.

13:10
Through insolence comes nothing but strife, but wisdom is with those who receive counsel.

13:14
The teaching of the wise is a fountain of life, to turn aside from the snares of death.

13:15
Good understanding produces favor, but the way of the treacherous is hard.

13:16
Every prudent man acts with knowledge, but a fool displays folly.

14:6
A scoffer seeks wisdom and *finds* none, but knowledge is easy to one who has understanding.

14:7
Leave the presence of a fool, or you will not discern words of knowledge.

14:8
The wisdom of the sensible is to understand his way, but the foolishness of fools is deceit.

14:12
There is a way *which seems* right to a man, but its end is the way of death.

14:15
The naive believes everything, but the sensible man considers his steps.

14:18
The naive inherit foolishness, but the sensible are crowned with knowledge.

14:24
The crown of the wise is their riches, *but* the folly of fools is foolishness.

14:33
Wisdom rests in the heart of one who has understanding, but in the hearts of fools it is made known.

14:35
The king's favor is toward a servant who acts wisely, but his anger is toward him who acts shamefully.

15:7
The lips of the wise spread knowledge, but the hearts of fools are not so.

15:12
A scoffer does not love one who reproves him, he will not go to the wise.

15:14
The mind of the intelligent seeks knowledge but the mouth of fools feeds on folly.

15:21
Folly is joy to him who lacks sense, but a man of under-

standing walks straight.

15:24
The path of life *leads* upward for the wise that he may keep away from Sheol below.

16:16
How much better it is to get wisdom than gold! And to get understanding is to be chosen above silver.

16:22
Understanding is a fountain of life to one who has it, but the discipline of fools is folly.

16:23
The heart of the wise instructs his mouth and adds persuasiveness to his lips.

16:25
There is a way *which seems* right to a man, but its end is the way of death.

17:2
A servant who acts wisely will rule over a son who acts shamefully, and will share in the inheritance among brothers.

17:10
A rebuke goes deeper into one who has understanding than a hundred blows into a fool.

17:12
Let a man meet a bear robbed of her cubs, rather than a fool in his folly.

17:16
Why is there a price in the hand of a fool to buy wisdom, when he has no sense?

17:21
He who sires a fool *does so* to his sorrow, and the father of a fool has no joy.

17:24
Wisdom is in the presence of the one who has understanding, but the eyes of a fool are on the ends of the earth.

18:2
A fool does not delight in understanding, but only in revealing his own mind.

18:4
The words of a man's mouth are deep waters; the fountain of wisdom is a bubbling brook.

18:15
The mind of the prudent acquires knowledge, and the ear of the wise seeks knowledge.

19:2
Also it is not good for a person to be without knowledge, and he who hurries his footsteps errs.

19:3
The foolishness of man ruins his way, and his heart rages against the Lord.

19:8
He who gets wisdom loves his own soul; he who keeps understanding will find good.

19:10
Luxury is not fitting for a fool; much less for a slave to rule over princes.

19:20
Listen to counsel and accept discipline, that you may be

wise the rest of your days.

19:25
Strike a scoffer and the naive may become shrewd, but reprove one who has understanding and he will gain knowledge.

19:29
Judgments are prepared for scoffers, and blows for the back of fools.

20:1
Wine is a mocker, strong drink a brawler, and whoever is intoxicated by it is not wise.

20:5
A plan in the heart of a man is *like* deep water, but a man of understanding draws it out.

20:15
There is gold, and an abundance of jewels; but the lips of knowledge are a more precious thing.

21:11
When the scoffer is punished, the naive becomes wise; but when the wise is instructed, he receives knowledge.

21:16
A man who wanders from the way of understanding will rest in the assembly of the dead.

21:20
There is precious treasure and oil in the dwelling of the wise, but a foolish man swallows it up.

21:22
A wise man scales the city of the mighty and brings down the stronghold in which they trust.

22:3
The prudent sees the evil and hides himself, but the naive go on, and are punished for it.

22:17
Incline your ear and hear the words of the wise, and apply your mind to my knowledge;

22:18
For it will be pleasant if you keep them within you, that they may be ready on your lips.

22:19
So that your trust may be in the Lord, I have taught you today, even you.

22:20
Have I not written to you excellent things of counsels and knowledge,

22:21
to make you know the certainty of the words of truth that you may correctly answer him who sent you?

23:9
Do not speak in the hearing of a fool, for he will despise the wisdom of your words.

23:12
Apply your heart to discipline and your ears to words of knowledge.

23:23
Buy truth, and do not sell *it, get* wisdom and instruction and understanding.

24:3
By wisdom a house is built, and by understanding it is es-

tablished;

24:4
And by knowledge the rooms are filled with all precious and pleasant riches.

24:5
A wise man is strong, and a man of knowledge increases power.

24:7
Wisdom is *too* exalted for a fool, he does not open his mouth in the gate.

24:14
Know *that* wisdom is thus for your soul; if you find *it*, then there will be a future, and your hope will not be cut off.

25:12
Like an earring of gold and an ornament of fine gold is a wise reprover to a listening ear.

26:1
Like snow in summer and like rain in harvest, so honor is not fitting for a fool.

26:3
A whip is for the horse, a bridle for the donkey, and a rod for the back of fools.

26:4
Do not answer a fool according to his folly, or you will also be like him.

26:5
Answer a fool as his folly *deserves*, that he not be wise in his own eyes.

26:6
He cuts off *his own* feet *and* drinks violence who sends a message by the hand of a fool.

26:7
Like the legs *which* are useless to the lame, so is a proverb in the mouth of fools.

26:8
Like one who binds a stone in a sling, so is he who gives honor to a fool.

26:9
Like a thorn *which* falls into the hand of a drunkard, so is a proverb in the mouth of fools.

26:10
Like an archer who wounds everyone, so is he who hires a fool or who hires those who pass by.

26:11
Like a dog that returns to its vomit is a fool who repeats his folly.

27:11
Be wise, my son, and make my heart glad, that I may reply to him who reproaches me.

27:12
A prudent man sees evil *and* hides himself, the naive proceed *and* pay the penalty.

27:22
Though you pound a fool in a mortar with a pestle along with crushed grain, *yet* his foolishness will not depart from him.

28:2
By the transgression of a land many are its princes, but by a

man of understanding *and* knowledge, so it endures.

28:26
He who trusts in his own heart is a fool, but he who walks wisely will be delivered.

29:1
A man who hardens *his* neck after much reproof will suddenly be broken beyond remedy.

29:3
A man who loves wisdom makes his father glad, but he who keeps company with harlots wastes *his* wealth.

29:8
Scorners set a city aflame, but wise men turn away anger.

29:9
When a wise man has a controversy with a foolish man, the foolish man either rages or laughs, and there is no rest.

29:19
A slave will not be instructed by words *alone*; for though he understands, there will be no response.

30:24
Four things are small on the earth, but they are exceedingly wise:

30:25
The ants are not a strong people, but they prepare their food in the summer;

30:26
The shephanim are not mighty people, yet they make their houses in the rocks;

30:27
The locusts have no king, yet all of them go out in ranks;

30:28
The lizard you may grasp with the hands, yet it is in kings' palaces.

31:26
She opens her mouth in wisdom, and the teaching of kindness is on her tongue.

About the Author

Dr. Steven Jirgal is the senior pastor of Lakeview Baptist Church in Monroe, N.C. He often serves as an instructional and motivational speaker to churches, civic groups, athletic teams, and business leaders. Steve and his wife Pam have been married for over twenty-eight years. They are blessed with three children, Joshua, Caleb, and Sarah. They make their home in Monroe, N.C.

OTHER BOOKS BY DR. STEVEN JIRGAL

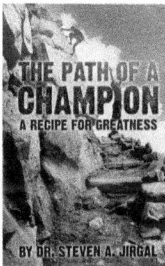

The Path of a Champion

The Dirty Dozen

Dying to Live

Life Points

Principles of Wholeness

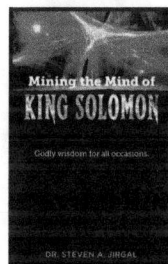

Mining the Mind of King Solomon

Questions regarding any of these titles can be directed to:
www.forerunnersinc@gmail.com

www.ingramcontent.com/pod-product-compliance
Lightning Source LLC
LaVergne TN
LVHW021524080426
835509LV00018B/2649